The Loudest Silence

My writings, you didn't know,
Were my cries for HELP!

By

Immane A Shiphrah

Chennai • Bangalore

CLEVER FOX PUBLISHING
Chennai, India

Published by CLEVER FOX PUBLISHING 2023
Copyright © Immane A Shiphrah 2023

All Rights Reserved.
ISBN: 978-93-56486-34-8

This book has been published with all reasonable efforts taken to make the material error-free after the consent of the author. No part of this book shall be used, reproduced in any manner whatsoever without written permission from the author, except in the case of brief quotations embodied in critical articles and reviews.

The Author of this book is solely responsible and liable for its content including but not limited to the views, representations, descriptions, statements, information, opinions and references ["Content"]. The Content of this book shall not constitute or be construed or deemed to reflect the opinion or expression of the Publisher or Editor. Neither the Publisher nor Editor endorse or approve the Content of this book or guarantee the reliability, accuracy or completeness of the Content published herein and do not make any representations or warranties of any kind, express or implied, including but not limited to the implied warranties of merchantability, fitness for a particular purpose. The Publisher and Editor shall not be liable whatsoever for any errors, omissions, whether such errors or omissions result from negligence, accident, or any other cause or claims for loss or damages of any kind, including without limitation, indirect or consequential loss or damage arising out of use, inability to use, or about the reliability, accuracy or sufficiency of the information contained in this book.

Table of Contents

I'm at my darkest   7

Paper Boats   8

Don't tell my Dad   10

She was   12

The Autumn leaf and wind   14

Suicidal   16

Me at my funeral   17

Head on the rails   19

Wounds   21

The day I drew the first line   23

She died alone   25

On the day She killed herself   28

Short lines   31

Belong   32

Love is blind.   33

Heart not head   34

What is depression   35

Good dreams   36

Home   37

A girl with Dreams   38

Full sleeves   39

To the overdoers   40

Cheers   41

Roaring   42

Wait   43

Depression 45

A Letter to the ones we lost 46

Life 48

A Wade through Lanes of Blood 50

Dear Depressed friend 52

Why are Angels always shown Roaming in the sky? 55

Dreamland's Wreck 57

UGLY 59

Faith 62

Reputation 64

Friends 66

Broken Church 68

Am I ? 70

Broken Toy 72

It's okay 74

Aren't we kids anyway? 76

A father's day poem   78

I Fell in Love   81

First Love   84

Two roads converged in the woods   86

The Middle   88

Human   90

The Falling Star   92

On My Knees   93

I didn't dare   95

She's not depressed   96

A pinch of sorrow in her tone   98

The page missing from my journal   100

Paradoxes   102

What If?   104

I'm at my darkest

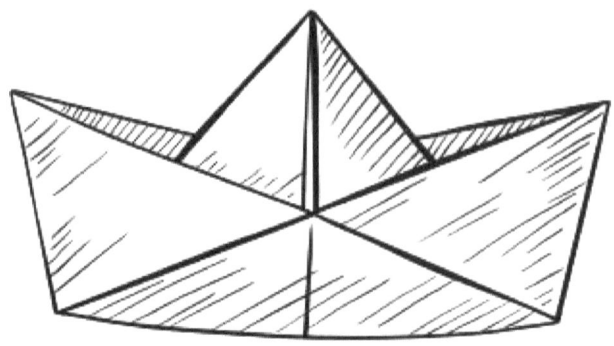

Paper boats

My being tattered,
Its tender skin ploughed with grief and agony.
My heart shattered,
My memoir filled with a never ending melancholic symphony.
"What a wonderful world!" Say you,
But ask me not, "what is life?',
To me, an ailing girl, life is blue, its wonders, a lie.
I am a little lady, sitting by a brook
Not I, a girl so steady, my foundations are shook.
Sat I there everyday,
Sending paper boats into the water,
Hoping they would reach the abbey,
Where the abbot is none but the father.
Wish I, my tender paper boats don't sink
'Cause it's a long way to go, and they carry what I think.
Insurmountable, the journey seems

So impossible, my prayers, to reach God, seem.
They won't get there, knowing it still, I kept sending my boats.
Isn't that in the storm, what is called, FAITH!
Believe I, the only way to keep my boats afloat!

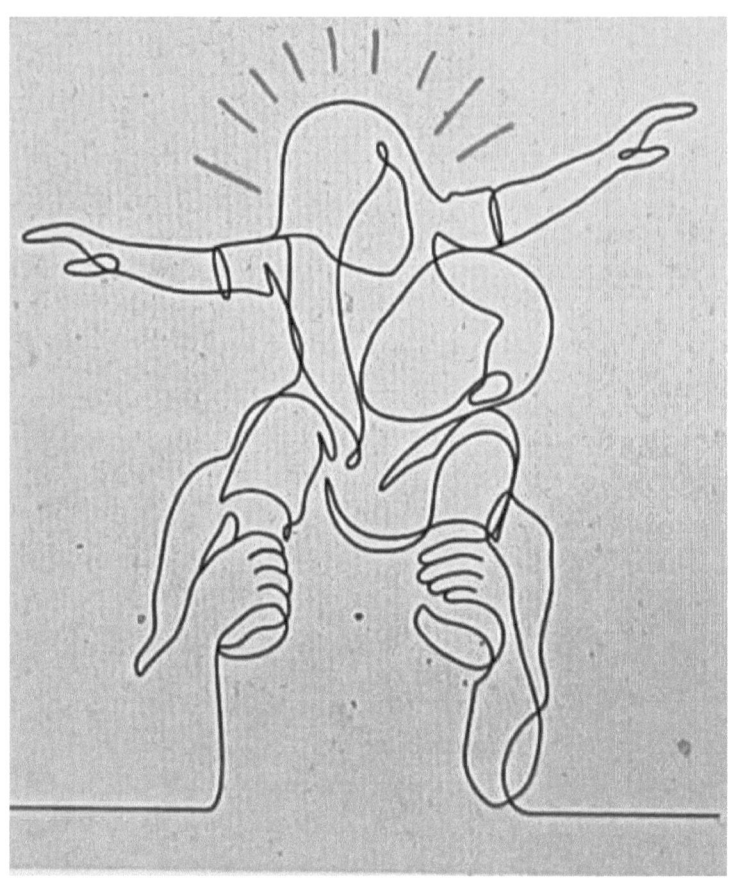

Don't tell my Dad

If you find me dead tomorrow
Please don't tell my dad ...
Without me he'd feel so hollow,
He would feel terribly sad...
He left me footprints to follow
But I was so scared.
Was succumbed to my sorrow

And was hurt pretty bad...
Drowned though the water was shallow...
Screamed for help, they thought I was mad..
I couldn't stand the deathblow,
Because no one really cared.
In pitying myself, I wallowed
Started hating everything I had...
Now that I'm letting my words flow,
After a long time I feel glad
But still I'm sinking below
The weight of the problems that constantly add...
I always hide what I undergo
Beneath a pretty, charming facade...
Now I'm feeling very low
I don't think there's a better plan
Than to leave it all here and go
Because my clock is lagged.
So I'll close my eyes 'fore it shows
Because it's too late, hurts too bad
I'm sorry I'm leaving tomorrow
Please take care of my dad!

She was

She was the little bird left behind by the flock,
She was the hour struck by no clock.
She was mystery personified,
She was history that never came to light.
She was the last piece of cake nobody ate
She was the last leaf hanging on an Autumn day.
She was the breeze hailing from the East
She was the beauty in the arms of the beast.
She was the missing piece we were searching for
She was the fill in void we were rooting for.

She was beauty in its perfection,
She was one rare creation...
Sadness was her name,
Without her, the world would be lame.
She might not be that great, maybe not the best,
To feel her, put your finger in the hole in your chest.
She is not someone distant; someone far
You can feel her as you run your fingers through your scars.
Do you still not understand that you are her and she is you
That sadness and despair, to you, ain't something new.

The Autumn leaf and wind

He walked in, the breeze on an autumn night
Making the leaves dance, left to right.
The radiant presence, what a beautiful sight
Every time he passed by, things felt right.
One leaf, to the autumn breeze asked,
"Would you be my man?", falling for that mask.
They held hands and took their oaths,
Oh, that green leaf, and wind in black coat!
She danced every time he passed by
But to him, she was nothing more than a passerby.

One cold night, when the leaf was sick
She lost her green, looked like a brownish brick.
She saw him coming from afar
She was overwhelmed with a racing heart.
But soon to her surprise, he pushed her down
She fell from the tree, like a queen's falling crown.
She screamed " WHY? ", he Laughed "WHY NOT?".
He said " you are just another dying fly, drawn to the flame hot.
You are just another leaf in this world of woods
To think you are my whole garden, you must be a fool."
Broken hearted the leaf died
But that's how most stories end, but it's a lie.
Yes, came the winter after,
She spent mourning with her soul shattered.
But she didn't take long to come back to life
'Cause she knew 'we all have battles to fight!'
Like a phoenix she began to sprout
Turned into a lady so strong and so proud!
I might not be the only leaf in your tree,
But I'm the only leaf, about whom the world now reads.
Broken trust, ailing relationships
Do break us, but only to fix.

Suicidal

Me at my funeral

Dear me,
There were times I helped others when they were down
But when it came to you, I pushed you away and let you drown.
I called you names I would never call anyone
I broke you down to build up some other one.
I was so hard on you, I never treated you right,
I never honored you, and told, you weren't worthy of life.

Many days, I tried to please others, letting you down
I never thought you had feelings and
Was furious with you for gaining every pound.
That night you walked into your room
I didn't know it was time I was going to be doomed.
I did see you write a letter to mom and dad
That you're leaving, begging them to not be mad.
You walked straight into the kitchen and took up that knife,
The tube light was glitching and so was your life.
Ran to your room and locked the door
I never thought you wouldn't walk out of it anymore.
Slit your wrists, one, two, three, four cuts
Blood started dripping, it flowed like a river of water.
What was I doing? Did I not say anything?
I'm ashamed to say it, but I was the reason behind everything.
I called You all bad things, and was so rude
That I was slowly, a bit by bit, killing you.
Then you laid on the floor, motionless, still
I then realized I should have put You first but instead I killed.

Head on the rails

I walked a mile to reach that place
On the way, a flashback of my days
Overcome with disgust I raced,
To that place that would set me free, I paced.
I hated how I looked, every part of me, oh my face!
I wasn't pretty enough nor did I hold that grace
I walked confused, as if I was caught up in a maze...
Fear, my only friend, depression embraced

Memories, too good and too bad, killing me equally, I can't erase.
All along I've been counting my days
Now it's time to finish my race.
I know tonight, I won't lie in a bed, but in a case
Don't mistake me for a girl who gave up, utter waste.
'Cause I did my best, until my last breath, happiness I chased
I'm going to a place on maps you can't trace
I'm going to leave behind a void nothing can replace.
I'm leaving, I need some space
I'm going home, my home awaits.
Too much pain, too much hate
Filled every moment, minute, every day
Reached...I waited at the spot to see who stays
But poor me, alone with loneliness disgraced.
Stepped on the track, put my head on the rails
Watched the train gain speed and towards me race.
In a moment, I'm gone.
An unwanted burden and piece of disgrace,
Finally left the world.
She can't be replaced,
she can't be replaced.

Wounds

Isn't it supposed to hurt,
When your skin is opened wide,
A knife sinking into your body
Stabbing straight into your chest, taking away your life.
Isn't it supposed to hurt
When the happiness you want, from you, hides
When you're no longer steady
And day by day, a part by part, you die.

Isn't it supposed to hurt
When blood oozes from your thighs
When you know you aren't brave
But still put on your skin that knife.
Oh isn't it supposed to hurt,
When in a dark room you lie
When the floor is bloody
And you're sad and don't know why.
Well, honestly, it doesn't hurt me
When I was low, darkness never left me.
I like the way it feels, to die everyday
I know I sound creepy, but the truth stays.
It's all that I've been feeling for a while now,
That I forgot what it felt like to be alive.
And the only way I know that I'm alive now,
Is 'cause it hurts and I'm not fine.

The day I drew the first line

The day I drew the first line on my skin
Showed me that the line between life and death was so thin.
I didn't know if I should feel proud or feel sad
'Cause that was my first attempt, and it wasn't that bad.
My hands were shaking, overcome by fright
Blood oozing from my cuts and tears barricading my sight
With no sound I was screaming for help
It felt like I shook hands with death at the doors of hell.

For a moment I thought I was dead
My eyes were closed, but could see a lot in my head
I saw devil making a deal with Jesus
Permitting him to tear my body into pieces
My guardian angel with his head bowed in shame
From the book of life erased my name.
I was taken down to a place of pain
Thrown into a pit full of monsters and was left there to remain.
Suddenly opened my eyes, the floor was stained
With the river of blood gushing from my veins.
Thought of calling my mom, but refrained
'Cause I know she'd sob and might even faint.
So with all my might walked out of the room
Blood dripping from my thighs, was nearing doom.
Was taken to the hospital in time and saved
But thoughts of not wanting to live, still stayed.
I know I didn't die that day
But a part of me, did fade away.
It still hurts but I choose to stay
'Cause the next line, I think, might take my life away.
This moment of fierce strife
Was also the moment that taught me life.
So the next time I hold a knife
I'll not let my thoughts run rife.
This little moment in time
Taught me what it meant to stay alive.

She died alone

3 am in the morning..
Still awake..
Too busy wiping blood off the marble floor…
Tried putting myself to sleep
Listening to some happy songs…
But that moment my heart broke
The moment I realized I was all alone…
Mom knocked the door

Hearing from my room, some weird noise..
"I'm fine mommy" shouted I from behind the door…
With tears dripping,
The ones that I couldn't hold…
"Got scared hearing a loud cry", she told
With relief seeing a smile I faked so bold…
5 am… still awake..
Called my friend because I was alone….
She didn't pick
Like I was someone unknown…
Called a few.. Ones I call 'bros'..
To see if they would respond…
Excused themselves saying
They were tired and put up a show…
6 am … still awake…
Took a bottle of pills just to say
Its too much for me to take…
And I'm broken beyond repair…
6:30 am….
Still waiting with love for someone to say..
That they love me too the same way…
But got a little dizzy …
7:00am still awake ….
My eyes started dimming..
But tried my best to wait,
For that someone who would make that day
A little brighter with the love they'd say…
7:30 am.. No longer awake…
Little by little started fading away…
Little by little dripping away…
I died still waiting for someone to say
"You are mine, I can't let you fade"….

That word was all I needed to stay awake…..
But poor me…I died alone
And died in pain…

On the day she Killed Herself

On the day she killed herself
They asked "why didn't she tell us she was
Depressed...??"
Well... She did...
She did when she told you she couldn't sleep and
was up all night..
When she spent an hour in the bathroom
And came out with baggy eyes...
When she wore full sleeves on a sunny day

And wouldn't let you know why....
When she wore skinny tight jeans
To stop the blood oozing from her thighs...
When she told you she wasn't feeling great
And sort of wanted to die....
When she sang songs that made no sense to u
But broke her and made her cry....
When she laughed so hard for a silly joke
Just to make sure she faked that smile...
When on phone, for a moment she held silence
And said it was a problem with the line....
When she said she was ugly and worthless
And would never be fine....
You thought it was modesty
But it was lack of self-respect that time....
She did, when that bottle of pills on the shelf went
Missing for two days and you just took it so light....
When she said she had nightmares
But you wouldn't care and let her die....
She did when she said she was happy
With a fake smile
That concealed a whole another
World where the days were nights....
When she said she was bullied for who she was
And what was on her mind...
But you.... You just let her slip through the cracks
of your cold embrace
And simply told her all will heal in time...
She did when she was in the bathroom
Holding up the blades...
Screaming for help and a warm embrace....
When she let the tub fill red and
The floor, all blood!

If these were not enough for you, WHAT WOULD BE????
She said it all ... Just that,
You didn't see...

Short lines

Belong

Sometimes people live in a home…
They think it's something they own.
But a few prefer to stay alone
Because they feel that's where they belong.

Love is blind.

Love is blind.
Because it takes you back to what hurt you.
Oh, to be more precise, love is kind.
It doesn't let another experience the pain that you went through.

Heart not head.

Then they all, together said
From her poems that they've read
If you want to hold her dead
You strike her heart not her head...

What is depression

They say "Depression is fighting with yourself.
The one who loses is still you"…
But oh Darling, one loses only when another wins.
Oh can't you see the winning other is YOU too!!!

Good dreams

I've heard of people being scared about bad dreams.
But am I the only person who can't stand a good one?
'Cause I think, a ghost staring straight into your eyes,
Is much prettier than seeing good dreams, you believed, die.
I wish my dream catcher, destroys good dreams too,
Just like it destroys bad dreams for you.

Home

I wept the moment I left home
I wept more when I realized I never had one.

A girl with dreams

She was a girl with a beautiful dream
But this awful world silenced her scream
She wanted to be the first of her kind
But the world thought she was out of her mind.

Full Sleeves

"I never knew she was suicidal"... They say..
Why in the world would she wear full sleeves on a summer day??

To the Over-doers

To all the overthinkers and overeaters
To the life haters, and wrist cutters....
To all the silent weepers and fake smilers...
To those drug users and addicted drinkers....
To the numb feelers and "can't anymore" sayers....
To all the tear eaters and blade users
There's hope ... Better day is on the rise....
You don't know it, but you're stronger
So keep pressing on ... Fight a little harder..
Put that music on, sing a little louder
Cause you are precious and you got to live a little longer....

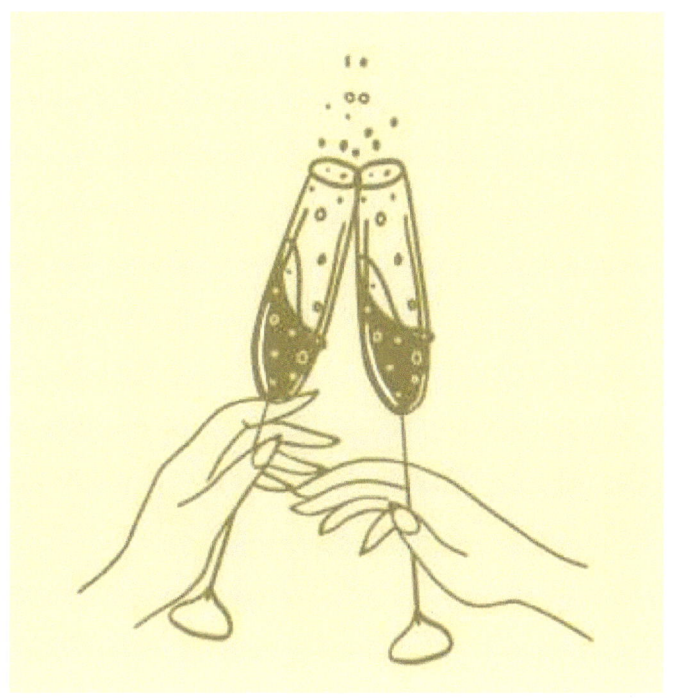

Cheers!

Cheers to the beautiful parts
Cheers to the broken hearts
Cheers to who we were
And to all the ones we cared...
Cheers to us and what we had...
To the broken past that we share..!

Roaring

That fighter in you may now be hidden too deep
Maybe for a while she has been asleep...
But remember, she'll come roaring like a lion one day
To slay all the enemies and brave the waves!
This mountain you climb might be too steep
But remember, the God above is watching your every deed
He's just waiting for the perfect day
To get you through and make a way!

Wait

I was once a girl with dignity and grace...
But now I feel like I'm losing the race...
Remembering all the good old days...
Trying to figure out my mistake
That lead to this battle that I now face...
I only asked for little space,
But you left, forever, and all I can do is gaze...
Wishing to once again be embraced
Or at least be let down paced...
Because, it's too hard for me to take
The fact that all your love for me turned into hate....
Waiting for a better day
Staying up, awake, so late...

Wishing to smile, once not fake..
A good life I'm trying to make
Out of this mess, rewriting fate!
I know for certain that one day
My life will be, of hope a ray
This is not my place to stay
I will keep fighting and all my life, wait!

Depression

A Letter to the ones we lost

I know how you would have felt
The moment you lay breathless
With your nerves breaking through your skin
With blood oozing from your wrists….
I know that moment, you wanted to stay alive….
But couldn't do anything but die ….
You were screaming your lungs out
Not because of physical pain

But because of the PAIN ….
Pain from the cuts, that the shattered
Pieces of your dream left.
You tried your best ….
You gave love generously
But it returned void. It failed to bring back the love you deserved.
The world was too cruel to treat you right.
I'm ashamed to say I was one of those who paid no
Heed to your inside's voice,
And considered your deadly cry, a fading noise…
Now that I stand at the same place, with nowhere to go…
Overcome by thoughts and letting emotions flow….
I realize I must have been there by your side
To hold your hand and tell you everything's going to be alright.
I'm sorry …. I didn't understand then,
What it felt to be miserably broken.
Now I'm here too. Maybe one day soon, I'll meet you…
Up there where we live … where we are given a chance to..
With love…
With cuts on arms and thighs ….
With deep regret of letting you slip by…..
Yours forever faithfully
A depressed teen.

Life

Travelling to a world afar
We spend days and nights
Some put their mind and heart
But some take it light….
For some it's a meadow walk
For some, an exhausting fight…
"Its not a big deal"
 I hear them talk
But Just because they say it, it isn't always right….
Ones that say it's dark
Are the ones that see the sky
But ones that see the stars

Are ones that see things bright….
Some try to put back broken parts
And put things back right
But some spend their time breaking hearts
With their bitter truth and luscious lies….
Some reach far
Far into the sky
Some end up scarred
Waging war against the tide.
Some rip apart
Some break and die…
But what are stars
But broken pieces in the sky.???
The moon has scars
But still it shines bright
Because the scars are what
reflect the light!!!
This is what I've known thus far
About a thing called 'life'
I'm not someone standing tall
And spreading light
I have my sails torn,
I'm Just another passer by….!

A Wade through Lanes of Blood

A forlorn stroll in the middle of a night
Deep through the thicket with no light
Jaded steps took I with fright
For the rest was still out of sight
Back turned I to read my story
From the ground that I floundered weary
The only figure saw I, clearly,
Was the dying me none bothered to carry

No foot prints of mine, far or near,
Just a longish trail of blood and tear
From the sheared body of someone dear-
The wrecked me before I reached here.
No change since the start,
Hurting inside and falling apart
Limping akin to a wounded hart
In the battle, killed I, a part of my heart
Still walking, ask me not why
For before the rains, face we, the dry
With hope of someone attending my cry
Someone to love me before I die
Though my memoir lacks meadow walks
And a million demons at my door knock
Breeding guts will I lug the spark
For death ain't my lane to park!

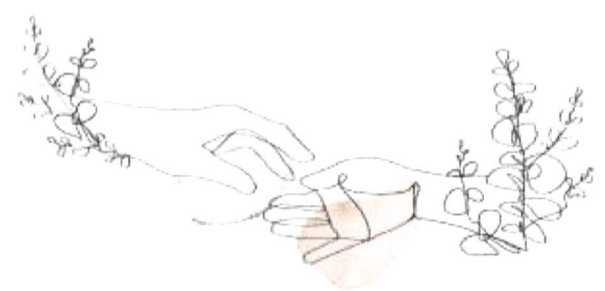

Dear Depressed friend

Friend,
It's getting harder each day to stand
Life sucks, things run out of hand
You don't know what to do.
Something hitting you
Hard inside your chest,
making it hard to take a breath…
Every night you cry yourself to bed
Turn the music high, to shut voices in your head.
From bright string lights, lanterns and bulbs
To a blue light dim and so dull

You change everything to see if it helps
How awesome would it be, if it changed what you felt..
You tried eating less, worked your best,
But found it hard to look like the rest....
You shared everything to everybody,
On your hunt to find somebody
Who would look into eyes,
Say darling you'll be fine.
But all that happened was, you were broken
Truth revealed and you were shaken.
People you once called friends, who became family...
You wonder "where did they go, when I needed them the most?"
People who seemed kind, people you believed
Were none but people who made you feel lost.
You're tired of it all, tired of all the lies..
Tired of all the songs, that sung the beauty of life...
All you needed was someone to hold you....
All you ever wanted was a hug to get you through..
But now you are tired, exhausted and broke....
So you came into your room with a pack of blades.
Started writing your story, and all the pain ...
Right on the tender paper skin...
Oh the lines of sorrow and despair win...
Then you became an artist on skin ...
Pain no more means anything...
Addiction overruled ... kicked out of school
Breaking apart... things got worse..
All you did was look for love, but ended up hurt
And now you want to end it all here...
But friend... you tried it all...

Would you listen one more time.
Darling you're beautiful just as you are…
With all the pain, the wounds and your scars.
Life isn't easy. I know it's hard…
But darling, remember you were meant to go far.
Better days are yet to come,
Stay strong, because you are the one…
You are stronger than you know, you were born to win…
Just shake it off your shoulders, straighten that crown
Oh princess! You are too high to be brought down..
You are loved… you are enough… you are beautiful…
You are brave…
You are worthy … you are strong….
Here, the night ends, face the dawn..
Now, I want to tell you…
You are such a great person…
I'm proud of you.
You made it this far. I'm sure you'll get through.
I believe in you.
Now throw away that pack of blades..
Darling you were meant to stay.
Even when you don't find a reason to.

Why are Angels always shown Roaming in the sky?

On the day the world was ending….
What a beautiful sight
Lovers loved more and held each other tight….
Lost love found in the dead of the night
Some screaming overcome by fright…
Bitterness vanishing in the blink of an eye
Every true love given new life…
That moment truth triumphed over all lies
And people to one another, were so very nice…
For a moment earth looked like paradise
Where people knew only to love and not to lie…
Running to their loved ones before they died
To convey their love one last time…
Expecting many, in a corner, stood I,
For a sweet embrace before I died
To hear "I love you "
Though a lie
I kept waiting all night…
Poor me…. I had to wait all night
Till, finally, I was embraced by the crumbling sky.

My body was shattered, my blood ran white.
Turned into an angel, shining bright.
Then I realized one thing that night
That the ones left alone and on their own died,
Were the angels that soared so high...
Then I learnt why,
Angels are always shown roaming in the sky
Running from court to court in the heavens high
Seeking justice and to be treated right!
Because they were all alone the minute they died
And they still remember that bloody night!

Dreamland's Wreck

Some said the day was bright
But no light there was in my sight
Oh the peace-wrecking bawl I hear
Of throbbing pain and dripping tear
Before I could process, fell in the night
For a doze, tried I, with all my might
Louder became that squeal of fear
Farther I ran, more I drew near
Took me not a shake to win the fight
Drowned I, asleep, into the bottom of the night
Popped up a land so familiar
Of authentic splendor, that to me was once dear

The tick I believed my haters right
Was when this world ran out of sight
Broken was I, learning it never was there
In front of me stands it, now, letting me stare
It took, like this, a night
To design this world of light
STOP! Lost in my world, do I now hear,
Oh that squealing screech of dread and fear?
Everything though wrong looks right
In this world lacking strokes of plight
Not a cry of anguish do I hear
Truly a land of my design, I swear!
To my woe, faded away that quick sight,
The darkest day rose from the brightest night,
A sound of shatter and pain did I soon hear,
The wrecking of the kingdom that to me was once dear.

.

UGLY

Maybe it's time I tell you who I am..
I'm not someone with proud curves.
Colored hair and those heavenly curls.
I ain't someone who looks great
Someone any boy would date.
I'm not someone with that contagious smile.
Nor am I someone who keeps up with trend and style.
I'm not someone who puts up photos for a dp....
I put up quotes saying I'm modest, to hide away the Insecurity...

I Don't laugh a lot Because I feel shy
As my teeth overlap one over the other, not being in a file...
I always tie my hair, I know I look old...
But my hair's so frizzy and I ain't so bold!
I'm not someone who smiles at the mirror
Instead I look at every flaw and call myself an error..
I think I'm good enough, but the moment I step out,
These voices inside my head start getting loud!
I'm not that girl with polished nails... Rather one with bitten edges...
I Don't style myself everyday, nor do I wear heels or wedges....
I have baggy arms and thick thighs
And I'm not the life of the party or the girl who gets high!
Rather someone left unnoticed who stands by the side
Wishing to be braver and little less shy.
I'm not great at dancing, I don't have special moves....
Just another girl staring at the floor with no clue......
But!!!!!
That doesn't make me any less a girl!!!
And I Don't have to have all of these to prove myself to the world!
Because I'm beautiful, even with all my bad looking days...
With chubby cheeks and glasses on my face ...
I am generous ... I've got love to give
And that makes me a human, I've got a reason to Live...!

Ponytail, braided hair, pimpled face and one so fair...
Aren't in any way different from each other
Because what's on the outside doesn't define what's inside
Her!!!
Cheers to all the too tall, too short... Too thin, too Stout...
Too light, too dark.... Too big, too small....
To everyone starving themselves just to look perfect...
U are already perfect .... Be you!
U are such an amazing person with a beautiful heart....
That's all that matters, the way you look does not!
You're the most beautiful person on the planet
With all that you are, just as you are!

Faith

I've heard many preach about Jesus…
They say, he is God most high, God of all seasons
Oh well here I am, ripping, breaking into pieces
And I know, for him to come, there's no better reason…
I recited the prayers, read the bible
I read about Jesus healing people
I wish he could heal me - one by her thoughts crippled
I wish he would meet me here, as I struggle….
I did trust God with all my self

It's not my fault that things didn't go well
But what's Faith? If you can tell….
Its belief strong enough to overthrow hell….
Here I am 19 years old
Too fragile. Fighting demons, I broke
Thinking a lot, with a little told
I'm afraid I'll die young, while I'm afraid of growing old..

REPUTATION

Sometimes it storms, sometimes it rains.
I don't know if you'd cry, but I'm sure you'd complain
These changes never fail to drive me insane….
Mental illness is not just a problem with the brain.
It can leave you alone in the night wiping blood stains
Off the floor, with a heavy chest laden with pain…
Depressed, bipolar, anxious…we are labelled a name

Here we stand together! There's a lot more we claim...
It breaks our heart to know that our efforts go in vain
How could you do this to us, without feeling a bit of Shame!
We are all untamed bulls guarded by chains
But we are so much more than what mere chains can contain
Through the ages, our dignity, we tried to sustain..
But there you go... tearing down our reputation all over again...

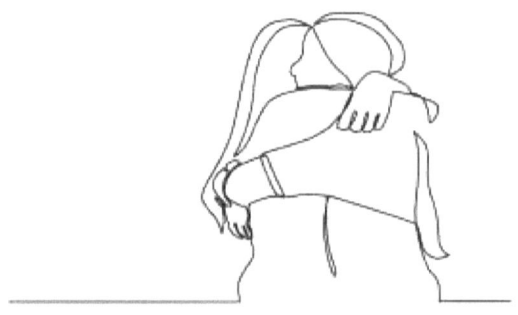

FRIENDS

I know neither of us was in good season.
We both had our so called 'trials'.
Though there were a million reasons..
Honey, I think we should have tried…
We should have given it a second thought
One last chance to our friendship.
Because we kept talking about who we were not
Forgetting about who we have been….
Those silly jokes only we could understand
The dirty side of us unleashed
We were one cool and lit gang
We took it to heights none can reach…
I still remember the agreement signed
That pinky promise made.
We promised to stay each other's side
Whatever be thrown our way…
Those sleepless nights with endless talking
Playing ghost games with your aunt

We never said the word boring
We had each other… what else did we want?
Today… looking back at everything
A drop of tear ran down my face …
Looking back at who we've been

Oh the gold old happy days…
Alas … we're strangers now…
But this time … with memories…
We parted not knowing how
But still loving each other dearly.
From diminishing text messages to nothing at all
From long conversations to a happy birthday call…
I can clearly see the relationship fading.
But let's do all that we can to stop its fall..
These days, every time I hear your name
I feel an ache in my chest.
Cuz you are my most treasured possession
You are my forever best !
They say,
When the sun dusks, conversations dawn…
It's almost night… I'm waiting for your call…
If you would give me one more chance
To tell you how much I miss you…
I promise I'll not leave again, stupid…
Because you are the most irritating person I know…
Still… you are the one I can't live without….

BROKEN CHURCH

Life isn't easy ... I know it's getting hard...
To know where you're going ... And to know who you are...
Just stop for a moment, look at your scars
Look at yourself... Look, you've come this far....
Don't give up now... Please Don't stop...
Addictions over rule ... I know it's hard...
Church ignored so you ran to the bar....
Cutting yourself .... Breaking your heart
Wrestling with demons and your own thoughts...
I know it isn't easy... Its tearing you apart....
You're doing all you can ... Giving what you've got
But everything you do never seems enough...
Recited the prayers ... Told verses that you knew...
Hoping God would come, hoping he would get you through...

Bible didn't seem to answer. So you thought there's no cure...
You struggled alone but what did the church do?
The elders of the church kept judging ...
They considered it all sin ... So they started Preaching....
Singing hallelujah and all the time praying
Is not going to get you to heaven unless you start reaching...
The church went preaching all night, all day...
But what did the kids of the church have to say?
You treated them as sheep gone astray...
And a little by little let them fade away...
Love is for all... That's what Jesus said...
Even for the one that is wanting to be dead...
For the Addicts of bottles and cigarettes...
Those at war with your thoughts lying on your bed!
Jesus loves you ... That's what the bible said...
Don't you remember the song that once got you to bed?
Not a boy, not a girl ... Who you are is still a question...
Oh dear child you are God's creation....
I understand the pain that you're going through.
No one understands. But remember, God still loves you.
Everything's going to be okay...
From The darkest of nights dawns the brightest of Days.
God loves you, that's all I have to say...
Keep fighting for you were born to stay!

Am I?

Am I the only person who privately weeps?
Who doesn't know to distinguish reality from dreams?
Am I the only one who's nothing I want to be
Or the only one who hears faith whisper and doubts scream.
Am I just another sinner redeemed

Or am I someone God holds dear?
If you'd throw me in an ocean I'm ready to sink
Already giving up, ready to leave...
Depression haunts... It's killing me ...
How long should I wait for god to intervene?
I constantly ask God "Are you playing with me ?"
If I'm useless to you, why don't you just dispose me!
You're the God most high, God of glory
But why would you hate me if I'm not who I'm supposed to be?
After all, I'm just trying to be me...
I'm yet to recover from slit wrists that bleed
Ashamed to call myself a misfit wanting to leave.
These thoughts rush in choking me,
Day by day its getting harder to breathe
God if I'm not what you need
Just let go of me ...
But I still know that one that I believe
He is Creator king God the Majesty.
But what was I made for? I Don't have a clue.
It leaves my heart scarred and my mind confused!
I'm just another sinner, I would never be a saint
Thought I'd never be the one God would never hate
But that's just a fake picture people paint
Jesus loves all, that truth'll never faint!
I know I'm meant to be, though I feel like a mistake
Because Jesus loves me and he wants me to stay!
This is just another poetry of a misfit misplaced...
I hope this would go far enough to reach heaven's gates!

Broken Toy

Shifting things from New York to LA..
I was too busy packing things, the whole day...
Kept some aside to throw away,
Those that were never meant to stay...
Something in the 'throw away' bin
Immediately caught my attention...
A fragile doll with a broken chin
With a face so dull and eyes so dim...
"I don't need it anymore"
I threw it away, out of the door...

Thought I can get a better one from the store,
Thought it meant nothing anymore...
Disposed the garbage, and now I'm on my way....
From New York to LA....
Something struck me hard that day.
That the doll was once the reason I smiled everyday....
He was once my best friend,
The one I made... My creation
I didn't mean to throw him away, that was not my intention.
I should have thought twice about his retention...
Peeped out of the window... Saw a garbage truck
Pass by and there was my little chuck...
My little boy was on that truck,
My little boy was on that truck,
That took him away to destruct....
On my way to LA.... The only thing on my mind was...
I shouldn't have left him... 'Cause he never did...
Broken and bruised... He still waited in the attic
For me to come back, and love him as I once did.
That broken toy wrecked my heart....
More truly, I broke his and tore him apart!

ITS OKAY

A quick reminder...
It's okay to feel broken ...
It's okay to not do anything,
Lie on your bed and stare at the ceiling...
It's okay to not feel okay...
It's okay if all that you did today
Was just fight your way through
Surviving the hard time...
It's okay to have scars ...
It's okay to shatter into a million pieces

Looking at someone's Instagram story ...
Looking at how happy they are ... And how happy You're not....
It's okay to cave in sometimes ...
Take some time for yourself darling, you deserve it...
It's okay to not fulfill your parents' expectations....
It's okay to not be a good friend...
It's okay to stay inactive on social media for a long Time....
It's okay even if nobody notice....
It's okay to have your mind go weirdly wild...
It's okay to mess up sometimes....
It's okay to stay confused and rip apart inside...
But oh dear... Remember one thing!
You are perfect just as you are and I'm proud of you!
With all that you've been going through..
The very fact that you are still alive and fighting, Is a hope that one day things will fall back into place ...
Don't take that extra step to hurt yourself ....
You deserve better .... Please Don't punish yourself...
You deserve the kind of love you give others....
I wish that one day you would want to stay alive Just as much as I want you to, right now....
The God is watching everything ...

Aren't we kids anyway?

Sometimes we act like we're grown up
Pretend to understand things
Turning major, doing drugs
We try to act cool.
But at the end of the party
With a glass of beer
Sitting on the sofa,
Have you ever felt it deep down
Does it make your heart inflate
Does this thought break your ribs...
Aren't we kids anyway?

We pretend to be strong and wise
We shower people with solutions for pain
We sometimes start to advise
While we ourselves are trying to not go insane
When you lie on your bed
And your room is dark
Thoughts running through your head

Heart beating fast
When all the grown up feeling fades
Do you hear a whisper,
Aren't we kids anyway?

Running behind an ice-cream van
Shouting in front of a pedestal fan
Still watching age old cartoon
Still laughing for silly jokes
Longing for amma's hug
Missing appa's guidance
Running into a stranger's arms
Trying to feel loved one more time..
Tell me, aren't we kids anyway?

A father's day poem

From those conversations on a bench in the park
To deep ones, that comes from the heart
My dad's been that one person listening to all my rants.

When I was a little girl
He was my whole world
He loved me more than I could ever imagine.
He's been there, from the start
He'll be there till forever falls apart
And he'll be there for me, no matter what.

Flashbacks of our little talks
Never fail to flood my mind
Whenever I think world's dark

He never fails to be my light.

I've been trying to be a good daughter
Since forever, to a perfect father.
I thought I was, but little did I know,
I wasn't even close.
I remember those days when we spoke of random stuff
From how beautiful the stars were,
To how the waves were so rough.

We spoke a lot, but long gone are the days
Now... Days blend into months, then into a pile of years of massive silence.
We don't talk a lot now.
Knowing pretty well, I'll never be the daughter I'm supposed to be.
How is he so perfect?
It Still remains a mystery.

We had great moments
Memories I'd never forget.
This love that ruled my heart
With time, became quiet.
My father's love, and mine for him
Crept to the back of my mind.
I gave up trying to please him
And starting chasing dreams to make the world mine.
But on this day, the subtle, surpassed the superior
On this day, the subtle proved supreme.
I'm glad that this day exists
So that we, the dad and daughter, don't die.

I'm glad we have a day in the year, to call, a father's time
Which teaches fools like me, that, without dads, love is a lie.

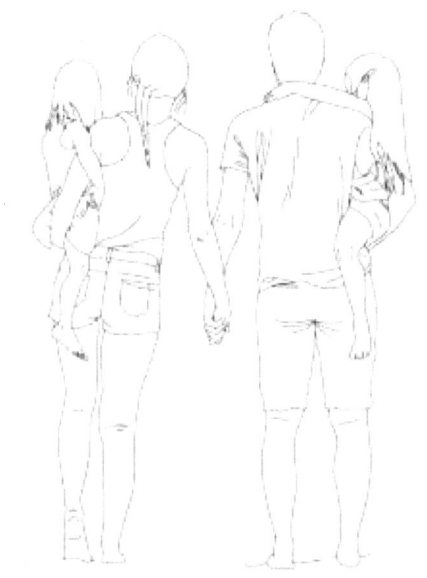

I Fell in Love

I didn't feel anything for a long time
Wasn't bold enough to cross the drawn line
My mind was bleak and my heart felt empty
I couldn't smile though the reasons were plenty
I tried everything I could to feel something
Maybe falling for someone, dating and dancing.
I wanted to feel the ground beneath my feet
I wanted to feel the smell of the flowers in the breeze.
Maybe love? Maybe hate?
Maybe smile? Or at least break...?
Maybe friendship? Maybe peace?
Maybe joy that'll never cease?

But I felt nothing, my mind was bleak
My heart went numb, my emotions leashed....
One day... Oh that one day
Everything had to change.
Walked into the bathroom with a pack of blades
Finally decided to let my being fade
That moment, something said wait
A reel, in front of my eyes, began to play.
For the first time ever, I could feel my heart beat
For the first time ever, I started to feel.
For the first time ever, I fell in love
Not with the handsome guy that lives next door
Not with the boy I met down the street
Not with the man, who's the conversation's heat.
I fell in love, with my mother.
With the way she holds me every time I cry, like no other.
I could see how much it would pain her if I leave
Why should I break her heart when all that she did was love me.
I fell in love. I fell in love with my daddy
With the way he looks at me when I sleep
With the way he puts up a brave face
Just to make sure I don't give up in the race.
I saw how much it would hurt him, if I die
He would feel hopeless and call God blind!
Why should I make him cry, when all that he did was make me smile ....

For the first time ever, I started to feel.
Threw that pack of blades away
Because that day I started to heal
And at least for my parents wanted to stay.

This is the story of how I dived
Into a pool of feelings, that night
Mom and dad held me tight
That moment, living never felt more right!

First love.

That was my first time falling in love.
I could hear my heart beat
Butterflies in my chest, and
Couldn't feel the ground beneath my feet.
I met beauty in person
Staring straight, not a blink

My heart raced,
I had a lot to say, but couldn't speak.
The very moment you see her,
You know she's someone you don't deserve.
Unsaid love and rejected feelings
Hurt more than pain can probably hurt.
The moment you let go,
The butterflies in your chest grow heavy.
There's this ache in your heart that words can't explain.
You can't do away with it
So you simply start romanticizing pain.
What is love if it doesn't kill?
Knowing Love is poison, we'd drink it, still.
First love tears you apart.
It cuts you piece by piece, stabs straight in your heart.
Then you live the rest of your life trying to forget
While reinforcing the same thing you want to forget.
When true love comes your way,
You'd still not want it anyway
The bird you let go
Still remains the prettiest
And its songs are the only kind of music
You'll ever move for.
Skies turn grey, life turns dark
Love, a game. The victim, your heart.
Though you pretend to not remember,
The first love, I think, will always be her.
Not just the first love,
But the love you'll desperately yearn to feel,
for the rest of your life.

Two Roads Converged in the woods

The road not taken, finally tried
Walking down that road is a thing of pride
But as I walked and destination arrived
There came a moment when my fascination died.
The road not tried and that often taken
Are always thought to end in different locations.
I chose the road less travelled by,
But it didn't make much difference.
'cause both the roads do collide

Standing at that point, I'm a witness of the convergence.
Doesn't matter where you travel as long as you are travelling
Because we're destined different places,
The truth is often hidden but now it's unravelling
We're putting back the pieces.
Choose the path you want to take
'Cause the decision is yours to make.
God will get you through even if you make a mistake.
'Cause he is not a God so cruel, so it doesn't matter which road you take.
In the end all who journeyed and all who tried
Are given a crown, and a seat by God's side.
Like frost was the witness of divergence
I stand here, as a witness of the holy convergence.

The Middle

There's black and there's white
But they say it's in the grey that life lies.
I always say it's either all or none
For me It's always been crawl or run.
The in-betweens never made sense
I thought they were between the extremes, a fence.
People notice the top and bottom
But the average is left unnoticed often.
Here I am fighting to reach the extreme
But living my life from the middle, it's only been a dream.
What are the in-betweens like?
Do the middle people have no life?
It took me all the time in the world to know
That it was the in-betweens that made us grow.
There is significance in the middle
Only the question and answer don't make a riddle.
It's the thinking in between that matters

When people don't realize, the middle shatters.
Though it took me long to understand
I'm glad I finally do.
I thought in-betweens kill, but that is where dreams brew .
Life happens in the middles
They make up most of our lives, though they sound little.
It's the in-betweens that cause a change
It's the middle-livers that set the range.

Human

You're not the only one
Who feels like the lonely one.
We all have struggles to face
We all grew from a rubbled place.
We are all ailing people
Who strive to be stable
We are torn into pieces
We've got our own reasons.
We're just strangers with a common scar.

We're just broken people with fragile hearts.
Our minds, an unbridled horse
Constantly unrest and always at war.
We wander the streets longing to belong...
Resting in a stranger's arms trying to feel home.
But also are we, pieces of heaven on earth
We move gracefully, not knowing our worth.
We are pieces of a puzzle, called to be an art
Oh in God's masterpiece we are all a part.
Beauty and poise we bear in our souls
And our body has no say in the life it holds.
We, are not the mistake but the solution
What others say of you is an illusion
We are the beauty that we need
We are the grace that we plead
We are the birds set free
We are more than what we see.
We are humans. We tend to feel down
We lose our voices and turn bound.
But oh you little human, things 'bout to turn around
Oh dear, it's time for you to unleash your sounds.

The Falling Star

Night sky with a falling star,
Wishing upon it, praying not to fall apart
Growing up hurts, my mom calls it an art
But I would say it's just an addition to your childhood scars.
But if you look into what you wish upon,
It's still a star that can't stop falling.
What can't aid its own, is no good for you.
So stop wishing upon stars
And try to find joy in your past
'Now' is all that you got,
Tomorrow can wait,
Try giving today a shot

On My Knees

Jesus, this time I'm here
Not with a list of blessings
But with a bottle of tears.

Jesus, here I come
Not as I was
But as who I've become.

Jesus, I'm in pieces
I don't know the reason
But I've got my doubts.

Oh Jesus, at your alter I have knelt
I'll sing your praises,
hope you hear the stories I have to tell

Walking down with my heartache
Eyes blurring with tears
Hoping to make it through someday
Hoping to face my fears
Jehovah Shalom, the keeper of peace
I pray you guard my mind, as I'm here on my knees.

I didn't dare

Well, I just came to say I no longer care.
The memories are haunting, they're a nightmare.
I came to say I no longer believe in prayer
And I also stopped believing life is fair.
I never took my eyes off you, I used to stare
But you didn't notice that I was even there.
This pain has turned to too much to bear
But this love of mine, I bet, is pretty rare.
You killed my soul, my life you spared
But to confess my love to you, I didn't dare!

She is Not Depressed

My lord!
I'm sure she's not depressed...
But I sure see some change...
Looks like she has regressed
From who she has grown to be, these days...
She says things weird; things too deep.
She says earth is a sphere, but the end is steep...
Her lips are sealed, but her eyes speak
The only time her lips open, is when she sleeps....
Oh when I think of this, shivers up my spine creep
I'm left without a clue, my mind is bleak..

These days she eats less,
Wears a 20 sizes larger dress...
But I don't think that is why,
Every time she goes out she feels shy...
She wears shirts with full sleeves..
But sir, I don't think there are cuts beneath.
She writes sad things
About losing the challenges life brings...
I asked her a million times, but she can't confess.
Maybe she has a hidden crimes she doesn't want to talk about, I guess...
She is not depressed sir. It's her fault.
She just changed a bit from her old ways.
I'm sure she's not depressed
But I sure see some change...

A Pinch of sorrow in her tone

There is a pinch of sorrow in her tone, sir..
The sunlight and little birds never failed to cheer her...
She finds no tone of grey when she looks at things
Her life is nothing but one massive colorful painting
With hues of yellow, saffron and red
Filled with glories the old tales said...
But lately my daughter talks in her sleep...

She talks of something, which is sure not counting sheep..
She speaks not in a familiar way
Not as cheerful as she speaks in the day...
When she wakes up, her eyes look alone
She eats less these days, that all I see is bone.
There's something wrong with her, sir
There is a pinch of sorrow in her tone ...

The page missing from my journal

I wish I had never met you
While I still keep staring at our pics.
I've many a times wanted to walk away from you,
But still, you're the only thing I cherish.
I sometimes regret being with you
But you are the only person who gives me chills.
I want to erase all the moments spent with you
The past haunts and memories kill.
You are the best thing that's happened to me, also the worst

We were interesting, but we wouldn't have
happened if I didn't move first.
You are a blessing and a curse
We made the perfect harmony like the rhyme with
the verse.
I don't know where we went wrong
That broke down our relationship, so strong.
It indeed pains me to know I'm no longer blessed
You're not here, there's no more of US.
We were broken people who needed love
And we found comfort in each other and it was
enough.
But now that life takes us to different places
It for sure hurts,
We all have different faces, and with time we
convert.
I Don't blame you... I'm not perfect too.
But I wish you see it inflicts me pain, more than it
does to you.
Cheers to the best part of my life
I really miss you, I'm not going to lie.
I thought our future was sealed, love eternal
But I didn't know that our future
will be the page missing from my journal.

Paradoxes

I wish you could see that I am a living mass of contrary ideas.
Sometimes I say the moon is beautiful while I despise enduring the darkness of the night.
I tell myself to hold on to hope while I know pretty well that it's going to stay this way forever.
I pray a million prayers though I least believe that they'll be answered.
Sometimes I'm in pain, the others, I yearn to feel it, but I turn numb.
Sometimes I hate being sad. The weight's heavy and it hurts pretty bad.

But sometimes I also start romanticizing sadness and wonder, "if not sadness, will I feel at all?".
Sometimes I cry in pain. My heart aches.
A hammer in my brain. But there are also times when I cause my own pain,
which tells me that I'm still alive and feeling.

I'm warm at heart, but I'm also cold sometimes.
My heart is soft, but it turns to stone sometimes.
I keep myself busy so that I forget to be depressed.
Yes it does the job, but it doesn't heal.

I am a north star guiding the ships home
But somedays I'm the storm, leading them astray.
Sometimes I feel lonely, that I start building my own kingdom,
my dreams are mine alone because I built them.
But then there are times I feel too much love, that it turns suffocating.
I dream for good things while I can't accept one.
Whenever blessing walks by, my mind hunts for the hidden curse.
Yes I am, a lady of paradoxes.
Sometimes I am and sometimes I'm not.
'What is' hurts and so does 'what's not'.

What if

What if life was easier?
Would it still be this beautiful?
What if darkness didn't exist?
Would the sunshine still be valued?
What if people didn't hurt?
Would they still be kind?
What if there was nothing to care about?
Would people still mind?
What if the birds don't fall?
Would they ever learn to fly?
What if wounds don't leave scars?
Would we be burnt and still look for fire?

What if hearts stopped beating?
Would they ever fall apart?
What if they feel too much?
Isn't that the point of having a heart?
What if no one dreams?
Would their thoughts ever go wild?
What if growing up didn't hurt?
Would anyone want to be a child?
What if, one day, the sun falls to the ground?
Would we even notice it?
What if the sky rips into pieces?
Would we still be busy minding our business?
What if humans did more than just exist?
Would they ever learn to live?
What if justice starts speaking?
Would the innocent still be killed?
What if happiness was given for free?
Would it be taken for granted?
What if parents understood their children?
Would they still feel abandoned?
What if life was less complicated?
Would it still be interesting?
What if there were no tears?
Would there still be oceans and rivers?
What if the fields grow weeds?
Would we still call the yield bountiful?
Oh! What if life was easier?
Would it still be this beautiful?

www.ingramcontent.com/pod-product-compliance
Lightning Source LLC
LaVergne TN
LVHW070940070526
838199LV00039B/723